COURTS OF APPEALS

GERALDINE P. LYMAN

PowerKiDS press.

NEW YORK

Published in 2020 by The Rosen Publishing Group, Inc.
29 East 21st Street, New York, NY 10010

Editor: Jane Katirgis
Book Design: Rachel Rising

Photo Credits: Cover sirtravelalot/Shutterstock.com; Cover, pp. 1, 3, 4, 5, 6, 7, 8, 9, 10, 11, 12, 13, 14, 15, 16, 17, 18, 19, 20, 21, 22, 23, 24, 25, 26, 27, 28, 29, 30, 31, 32 Allgusak/Shutterstock.com; p. 5 Lisa S./Shutterstock.com; p. 6 wavebreakmedia/Shutterstock.com; pp. 7, 13 Hero Images/Hero Images/Getty Images; p. 9 Steve Heap/Canopy/Shutterstock.com; p. 9 (insert) PJF Military Collection/Alamy Stock Photo; p. 10 ALPA PROD/Shutterstock.com; p. 11 fizkes/Shutterstock.com; pp. 12, 14, 20, 22, 26, 28 AVA Bitter/Shutterstock.com; p. 15 https://commons.wikimedia.org/wiki/File:New_York_Court_of_Appeals_hearing_oral_arguments.jpg; p. 16 Tolikoff Photography/Shutterstock.com; p. 17 Thorney Lieberman/Photodisc/Getty Images; p. 19 https://commons.wikimedia.org/wiki/File:Vermont_Supreme_County_Building_August2014.jpg; p. 21 https://upload.wikimedia.org/wikipedia/commons/2/26/053107-5thCircuit.jpg; p. 23 Tono Balaguer/Shutterstock.com; p. 25 Bettmann/Contributor/Getty Images; p. 27 https://commons.wikimedia.org/wiki/File:Supreme_Court_of_the_United_States_-_Roberts_Court_2017.jpg; p. 29 Win McNamee/Getty Images News/Getty Images; p. 30 Guzel Studio/Shutterstock.com.

Cataloging-in-Publication Data

Names: Lyman, Geraldine P.
Title: Courts of appeals / Geraldine P. Lyman.
Description: New York : PowerKids Press, 2020. | Series: Court is in session | Includes glossary and index.
Identifiers: ISBN 9781538343166 (pbk.) | ISBN 9781538343180 (library bound) | ISBN 9781538343173 (6 pack)
Subjects: LCSH: Appellate courts--United States--Juvenile literature.
Classification: LCC KF8750.L959 2019 | DDC 347.73'8--dc23

Manufactured in the United States of America

CPSIA Compliance Information: Batch #CSPK19 For further information contact Rosen Publishing, New York, New York at 1-800-237-9932.

Contents

THE U.S. JUSTICE SYSTEM

All around the world, governments have laws that explain what people, companies, and organizations can and can't do. These laws are carried out by justice systems. An important part of a justice system is the court system. Courts are places where people talk about whether or not a law was broken and what the outcome of legal cases should be.

In the United States, there's a dual court system. This means that there's a federal court system and a state court system. Federal courts deal with laws at the nationwide level. State courts consider state laws and can be broken down into smaller, local courts. In each system, however, there are many types of courts. There are criminal courts, civil courts, and courts of appeals. Let's take a closer look at these courts.

Courts are an important part of federal, state, and local governments.

THE MANY TYPES OF COURTS

Most people are familiar with criminal courts. These courts decide if one person broke the law. The next most common courts are civil courts. Civil courts work with people who claim another person or group failed to treat them properly. Third, there are the courts of appeals.

In criminal courts, lawyers present evidence and ask witnesses questions.

Courts of appeals are a bit different from the other two courts because a person doesn't go on trial. Instead, courts of appeals look at previous cases. They make sure that the police, lawyers, and judges who ruled on a previous case followed all the laws. In this way, a court of appeals puts the previous case on trial. Courts of appeals are a very important part of the legal process and an **essential** part of the U.S. government.

7

APPELLATE COURT DIFFERENCES

Courts of appeals have a different process than criminal or civil courts. The job of an appellate court is to **evaluate** previous trials. Therefore, no new information can be added to the cases. That means no new evidence or facts can affect the outcome.

Another important difference is that there is no jury. Instead, there are multiple judges. These judges make up a **panel**. Together, they make sure that all laws were followed during the case. For example, they make sure that all evidence presented was admissible, or able to be used in court. They also decide whether or not the outcome was correct. These judges think about whether or not a person was at fault. They can determine if a **sentence** is too long.

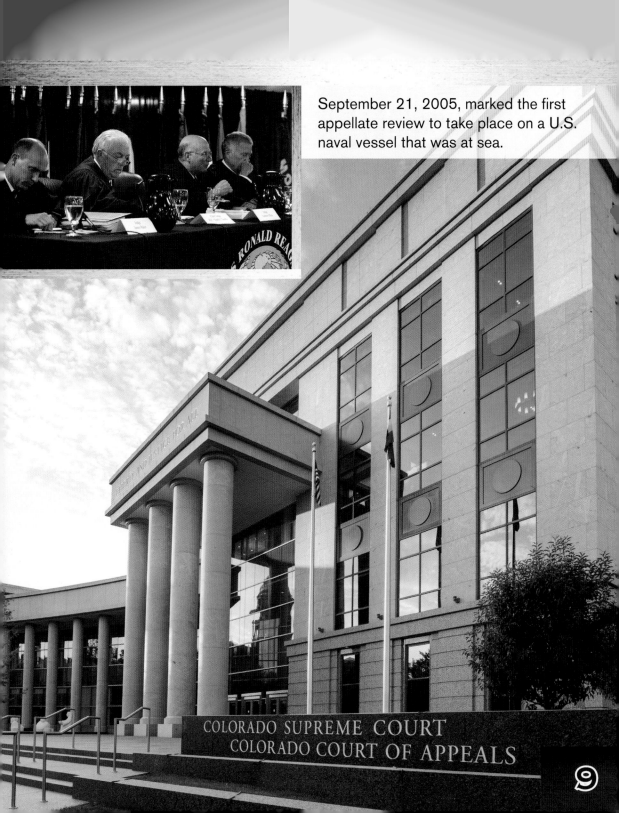

September 21, 2005, marked the first appellate review to take place on a U.S. naval vessel that was at sea.

COLORADO SUPREME COURT
COLORADO COURT OF APPEALS

WHO GOES TO APPELLATE COURT?

All people appealing a case have already been to trial in either criminal or civil courts. However, not all people who went to court file for an appeal. Only people who don't agree with the outcome of their case make this next step.

In many situations, a petitioner and their lawyer have to file an appeal within 30 days of the previous court decision.

If a person decides to ask for an appeal, there are specific time limits to make sure the appeal is addressed quickly. The first step in the appeals process is to file a request for appeal. This is a request to have a case heard by a court of appeals, or appellate court. If this person is granted an appeal, they are then referred to as the "**petitioner**." Other names for a petitioner are "appellant," "pursuer," or "plaintiff in error."

WRITING A BRIEF

Once an appeal has been approved, the petitioner's lawyer will write a **brief**. There are several kinds of legal briefs, but for courts of appeals, a lawyer bringing the case will file an appellate brief. This is the most important **document** for the petitioner. An appellate brief will contain the argument that the lawyer is presenting to the judges. It includes laws and decisions that support the position the lawyer is taking.

The opposing lawyer represents the **appellee**. This lawyer will write their own brief defending the previous trial and its outcome. This opposing brief is

Amicus Brief

Sometimes briefs are filed for a case by an amicus curiae, which is Latin for "friend of the court." People or organizations who have a strong belief that a side of an appellate case is right can file briefs to add to the case's argument. The amicus curiae brief will include arguments and any information to try to influence a case's outcome. Even though they file briefs, an amicus curiae isn't

NOT SO "BRIEF"

Even though they're called "briefs," which means "short," these documents can be quite lengthy—sometimes they're thicker than textbooks!

A lawyer spends a lot of time working on a brief that will make a strong argument to the court.

called a response brief. After the response brief is filed, the petitioning lawyer will sometimes respond with a third document called a reply.

GOING TO COURT

After all the briefs are written and filed, judges are assigned to the cases. They read all the briefs and replies. Then it's time for a hearing.

A hearing brings the petitioner, the appellee, their lawyers, and the panel of judges together. The lawyers then make their arguments aloud. Judges ask questions about the case. Often these questions take up most of the time during the hearing.

After the hearing, each judge carefully considers the case. They think about all the arguments they have heard. Then they come to a decision. Often, judges will

Dissenting Opinions

Sometimes judges on the panels don't agree with one another. In this case, a majority of the judges decides the case. However, if a judge feels very strongly, they may write a dissenting opinion. Dissenting opinions don't change the outcome of the case. Instead, they can provide more information for judges making

Lawyers give oral arguments, which means they review their arguments out loud to a panel of judges.

talk with each other, which can help them understand the case better. Finally, one of the judges writes the panel's decision. This decision is called the opinion.

AFTER THE OPINION

   Opinions can have big consequences. Suppose the judges find there was a problem with the first trial that affected the outcome of the case. Their opinion can reverse the original decision. If they find no problems with the first trial, they will **affirm** it, and the previous decision stays. Sometimes the petitioners are happy with the outcome, and sometimes they're disappointed.

   Can you appeal an appeal? The answer to this is a little difficult. In most states, everyone has the right to the first appeal. This is called the appeal "as of right." Once a court of appeals makes a decision on the first appeal, however, it's up to the courts whether or not the case deserves a third, fourth, or fifth chance.

SECOND TIME AROUND

After the first appeal, the next appeals are called discretionary appeals.

APPELLATE COURT
BOONE COUNTY, WEST VIRGINIA

STATE COURTS OF APPEALS

The majority of court cases in the United States are dealt with on the state level. Cases that deal with state laws, and disagreements and crimes that happen within a state, are state cases. There are 50 different systems for appeals, one for each state.

For example, in the state of California, there are trial courts, six appellate courts, and one supreme court. The six appellate courts are divided by region. These are the first round of courts of appeals. If a case is appealed again, it goes to the state supreme court. On the other hand, in Vermont, there are many different types of trial courts: civil, criminal, environmental, family, and **probate** courts. However, there is no in-between step. Every appeal from these courts is heard by the Vermont Supreme Court.

The Vermont Supreme Court is located in Montpelier, Vermont, and has a panel of five judges.

111 STATE ST.

111 STATE STREET

VERMONT SUPREME COURT
COURT ADMINISTRATOR
ENTRANCE FOR 111 AT 109 SIDE
DOOR, OFF GOVERNOR DAVIS AVE

FEDERAL COURTS OF APPEALS

District courts deal with federal cases. Federal cases deal with the U.S. Constitution and U.S. laws and treaties. They also look at disagreements between people across state lines and cases that involve **habeas corpus** rights.

To appeal a district court case, the petitioner must go to the federal courts of appeals. There are 13 courts of appeals divided up by region into circuits, plus the U.S. Supreme Court. Before the federal courts of appeals were created, the Supreme Court had to

Habeas Corpus

Habeas corpus is a legal process and a right to protect citizens from illegal imprisonment. When the government keeps a person in prison or a **detention** center, that person has a right to request that the federal courts examine why they're locked up and if

JUDGES IN THE PANEL

The Evarts Act established a three-judge panel for the federal courts of appeals: a circuit justice, a court of appeals judge, and a district court judge. Each judge's experience brings a different point of view to the case.

The United States Court of Appeals for the Fifth Circuit is housed in the John Minor Wisdom U.S. Courthouse in New Orleans, Louisiana.

address all appeals at the federal level. This worked for many years, but as time went on, it became clear that there were too many cases for the Supreme Court to handle. In 1891, the Evarts Act created the circuit courts of appeals.

GETTING TO THE SUPREME COURT

The U.S. Supreme Court is a very special court. It's a bridge across the dual court system, and it can look at both state and federal cases. However, it is a long path to the most respected panel of judges in the United States.

Suppose a case took place at the state level. This case must first be appealed through appellate courts in the state, including the state supreme court. After that, lawyers may ask that the U.S. Supreme Court hear the case.

How Many Cases?

Lawyers ask the U.S. Supreme Court to review more than 7,000 court cases each year. The court only hears about 150 of those. Though these sound like big numbers, in 2016 federal district courts reviewed over 350,000 cases—and that doesn't

LEGAL LINGO

Lawyers must file a petition to have a case considered by the U.S. Supreme Court. This is called a petition for a writ of certiorari.

The U.S. Supreme Court is the final court of appeals.

If the case was at the federal level, it must be heard in the district courts, then heard by one of the 13 circuit courts. After that, the person who has lost the case may choose to ask the U.S. Supreme Court to hear it.

TINKER V. DES MOINES

One example of a federal case that went all the way to the Supreme Court is *Tinker v. Des Moines*. In 1965, three students decided to protest the Vietnam War by wearing armbands. The Des Moines, Iowa, schools decided to suspend students wearing the armbands to prevent a disturbance.

Because this issue dealt with the First Amendment, *Tinker* became a federal case. The district court decided that it was reasonable to suspend the students in order to prevent disturbance. Unhappy with the case, the students' parents appealed. The case went to the U.S. Court of Appeals for the Eight Circuit, but the court was split, which upheld the earlier decision. The case went to the Supreme Court in 1968. In 1969, the court decided the students had a right to protest and shouldn't have been suspended.

FIRST AMENDMENT

The First Amendment protects the right of people to protest with symbolic speech, such as wearing T-shirts or armbands to support a political cause.

The students wore armbands to show that they didn't agree with U.S. involvement in the Vietnam War.

THE HIGHEST COURT IN THE LAND

The United States Supreme Court is the highest court in the United States. It's located in Washington, D.C. Throughout history, the Supreme Court has had as few as six justices and as many as ten. Today, the Supreme Court has nine justices: eight associate justices and one chief justice. Each justice on the Supreme Court has been nominated by the U.S. president and then confirmed by the U.S. Senate.

Becoming a Supreme Court Justice

The president of the United States is the only person who can nominate someone to be a Supreme Court justice. This is part of the system of checks and balances in the U.S. government. There are many other judges who are nominated by the president, as well. There are more than 600 judges on the district courts and 200 on the federal courts of appeals. The president nominates someone for every

Justice John Roberts is currently the chief justice of the U.S. Supreme Court.

The Supreme Court is special because it is a trial court and an appellate court. It hears cases dealing with disagreements between states and cases dealing with government officials. However, it is also the final court of appeals for the United States. The U.S. Supreme Court reviews very few appellate cases, but those cases can have big consequences.

THE POWER OF THE JUDICIAL BRANCH

There are three branches of government in the United States: the legislative branch, the executive branch, and the judicial branch. Each of these branches has checks and balances to make sure no one branch gains too much power. The Supreme Court is the head of the judicial branch. The Supreme Court's role as a court of appeals is important in part because it has a power called judicial review. This power is an important balance to Congress's ability to create laws and the president's ability to create executive orders.

Harper v. Virginia Board of Elections

On more than one occasion, the Supreme Court has struck down laws with its power of judicial review. One example of this was the case *Harper v. Virginia Board of Elections* (1966). In this case, Anne Harper wasn't allowed to register to vote because she didn't pay a poll tax. When the case came to the Supreme Court, the justices decided that poll taxes go against the Constitution. The decision banned state poll taxes across the nation.

THE HISTORY OF JUDICIAL REVIEW

Judicial review isn't part of the U.S. Constitution. The case *Marbury v. Madison* in 1803 established this power.

People sometimes protest to show support or opposition for major court cases.

Judicial review is the power to overturn a law or executive order that the Supreme Court decides is unconstitutional. This means that, in an appeal, the Supreme Court can decide whether or not a law or executive order is legal at all. It is an amazing power that has shaped U.S. history.

IMPORTANCE OF APPEALS

Courts of appeals hold the law and the people who enforce it to the highest standards and **ethics**. Appeals are very different from other trials—they lack the drama shown on television shows. Without witnesses or juries, it may seem like a type of law that's very separate from our day-to-day lives. Yet appeals can make a huge difference to those whose court cases get reversed—or their sentences changed. Appeals are where a lot of lasting change can happen. They can even affect the way laws are carried out. Only the Supreme Court has the right to review whether or not a law is constitutional, and that's a truly powerful part of what makes the U.S. government work.

GLOSSARY

affirm: To declare that the previous decision stands.

appellee: The person or party who's won a case that's now under appeal.

brief: A legal document that states the facts a lawyer plans to use in a court case.

detention: The act of keeping someone in prison or another place, or the state of being kept in such a place.

document: A formal piece of writing.

essential: Necessary.

ethics: Rules based on what's right and what's wrong.

evaluate: To study or assess.

habeas corpus: A legal right and process to determine whether a person can be held by the government.

panel: A group of judges that reviews cases in the courts of appeals.

petitioner: A person who applies to a court for an appeal or another court action.

probate: Having to do with proving in court that a last will is real and acceptable.

sentence: The punishment given to a defendant found guilty in court.

INDEX

WEBSITES

Due to the changing nature of Internet links, PowerKids Press has developed an online list of websites related to the subject of this book. This site is updated regularly. Please use this link to access the list: www.powerkidslinks.com/courts/appeals